DISCOVERING THE
INCA
ICE MAIDEN

MY ADVENTURES ON AMPATO BY JOHAN REINHARD

■ NATIONAL GEOGRAPHIC SOCIETY

WASHINGTON, D.C.

Published by the
National Geographic Society
1145 17th St. N.W.
Washington, D.C. 20036

Reg Murphy,
President and Chief Executive Officer

Gilbert M. Grosvenor,
Chairman of the Board

Nina D. Hoffman,
Senior Vice President

William R. Gray,
*Vice President and
Director of the Book Division*

Staff for this book:

Barbara Lalicki,
Editor

Marianne R. Koszorus,
Senior Art Director

David M. Seager,
Art Director

Carl Mehler,
Senior Map Editor

National Geographic Maps
and Jehan Aziz,
Map Production

Christopher A. Klein,
Map Artwork

Jennifer Emmett,
Assistant Editor

Meredith D. Wilcox,
Illustrations Assistant

Anne Marie Houppert,
Indexer

Vincent P. Ryan,
Manufacturing Manager

Lewis R. Bassford,
Production Manager

Cover:
*This Inca girl was sacrificed over 500
years ago. She's seen here against the
backdrop of the Peruvian Andes.*

Title page:
*Johan Reinhard and the Inca ice maiden
in a laboratory at Catholic University in
Arequipa, Peru.*

Library of Congress
Cataloging-in-Publication Data

Reinhard, Johan.
        Discovering the Inca Ice Maiden :
my adventures on Ampato / by Johan Reinhard.
            p.   cm.
        Includes timeline, glossary, and
index.
        Summary: A first-person account
of the 1995 discovery of the over 500-year-
old Peruvian ice mummy on Mount Ampato
and a description of the subsequent retrieval
and scientific study.
        ISBN 0–7922–7142–4
        1. Incas—Antiquities—Juvenile
literature. 2. Mummies—Peru—Ampato,
Mount—Juvenile literature. 3. Reinhard,
Johan—Juvenile literature. 4. Archaeol-
ogy—Methodology—Juvenile literature. 5.
Peru—Antiquities—Juvenile literature. [1.
Incas—Antiquities. 2. Mummies—Peru. 3.
Reinhard, Johan. 4. Peru—Antiquities. 5.
Indians of South America—Antiquities. 6.
Archaeology.]
I. National Geographic Society (U.S.) II.
Title.
F3429.3.M8R45   1998
985'.019—dc21   97–31291
                                        CIP

All photographs are © Johan Reinhard
except those on pages 6-7, and 36, by
Stephen L. Alvarez.

Johan Reinhard took the photograph
on page 13, which gives a clear view of the
summit, during the second expedition.

The illustration on page 37 is by
Christopher A. Klein,
National Geographic Artist.

C O N T E N T S

Sabancaya became increasingly active during 1990, erupting about half a dozen times a day—every day of the year. The erupting volcano spewed clouds of dark ash up into the sky. Wind carried the ash over Sabancaya's higher neighbor, the volcano Ampato, which is inactive. Eventually Ampato's snow-capped summit was covered with dark ash, which slowly began absorbing the sun's rays, causing the snow to melt.

After four years the weight of the melting snow caused a section of Ampato's highest summit to collapse into its crater.

Within this mix of falling ice and rock was a cloth-wrapped bundle.

When the bundle smashed against an icy outcrop about 200 feet below, an outer cloth was torn open—and 500-year-old Inca artifacts were strewn over the rugged landscape.

But the most important part of the bundle remained intact as it came to rest on top of the ice. It was the frozen body of an Inca child. Now a race against time began. Before long the body could be destroyed by the sun and volcanic ash—or stolen by treasure hunters.

The volcano Sabancaya erupts, sending a cloud of ash over a mile into the sky (left and above). The volcanic ash is carried by the wind over the taller mountain, Ampato (above, right).

5

As you can see in this photograph of me climbing Ampato, volcanic ash from Sabancaya has darkened the snow. The darkened snow absorbs heat from the sun, causing it to melt.

I'd climbed more than a hundred volcanoes in the Andes mountains without ever seeing an active volcano up close. From the top of Ampato, I would be able to look down and see Sabancaya erupting. I was excited as my Peruvian assistant, Miguel Zárate, and I started our climb out of the village of Cabanaconde, heading toward Ampato. On September 5, we made a small base camp at 16,300 feet.

Mountains have fascinated me since I was boy growing up in the flat plains of Illinois. As soon as I was able to get into the mountains at age 18, I began learning how to climb the steepest

routes. Before long I was scaling the highest peaks in Europe. In my mid-20s I began climbing in the Himalayas of Nepal and was a member of an expedition to Mount Everest, the world's highest mountain. At the same time I became an anthropologist who studies ancient cultures.

My two main interests merged in South America.

In Peru, Chile, Bolivia, and Argentina there are more than 50 ancient ceremonial sites high in the Andes, above 17,000 feet. All of them belong to the Inca culture.

The beauty and extreme ruggedness of the mountains at such altitudes appeals to me as a climber, while the mysterious Inca ceremonial sites attract me as an anthropologist.

eruvian women at a ceremony involving mountain worship near Cuzco, the center of the Inca empire (upper left). Two Peruvian women walk beside a beautifully carved Inca stone wall in Cuzco (lower left).

Incas began expanding their reign outside their homeland in the highlands of central Peru over 500 years ago, around A.D. 1438. Before the Spanish conquest of A.D. 1532, the Incas had created an empire that extended over 2,400 miles from the Colombian border to central Chile.

It was the largest empire established in the Americas by native people, and covered an area roughly equal to the distance between the western and eastern coasts of the United States.

The Inca Empire became renowned throughout the world for a number of reasons. The Incas built one of the ancient world's most extensive road systems. The richness of their culture is seen in the fine craftsmanship of their pottery, textiles, and metal sculpture.

Architectural achievements—such as the mysterious ruins of

Machu Picchu—continue to amaze us. In many cases, Inca stonework was so finely done that even a knife blade cannot pass between the carved blocks.

The Incas also made massive terraces for farming and storage facilities that allowed them to preserve their agricultural surpluses for times of need.

The materials left behind by the Incas at high altitudes in the Andes are well preserved by the cold. And looters find these sites difficult—though not impossible—to get to.

This means that we can often discover pottery, jewelry, sculptures, and other cultural artifacts "in context"—just as the ancient peoples left them.

It seems as if the Incas left the artifacts behind on the mountain only moments ago. The past feels like the present and becomes vividly alive.

Machu Picchu was one of the few Inca sites to escape destruction by the Spanish conquistadors. Discovered in 1911, it is still South America's main tourist attraction.

During our first ascent of Ampato on September 6, we made our way up the northern slope. We thought this would be a fairly simple route, but, as we neared the top, ice pinnacles blocked our way. They had been formed by erosion caused by the sun and wind.

We had to break through a mile of ice pinnacles to reach one of the lower summits at 20,400 feet. Much to our surprise, just as we were about to reach it, we saw a long layer of grass encased in the ice. We were puzzled. How did so much grass get here? Grass could not grow at this altitude!

We climbed the rest of the way to the summit and found that it was rounded and covered with grass, the "grass site." Pieces of Inca pottery and textiles, rope, chunks of wood, and even leather and wool sandals were scattered about. Flat slabs of rock had been carried from over a thousand feet below to make flooring. One slab still had a rope around it. The rock floor had been covered with thick layers of grass, to make a resting place.

Llama feces were scattered about. They indicated that over 500 years ago the Incas had used these animals to bring supplies up the mountain. Altogether the llamas must have carried up tons of material.

Miguel points to a layer of dead grass on Ampato. The grass had been growing about a mile below, over 500 years ago.

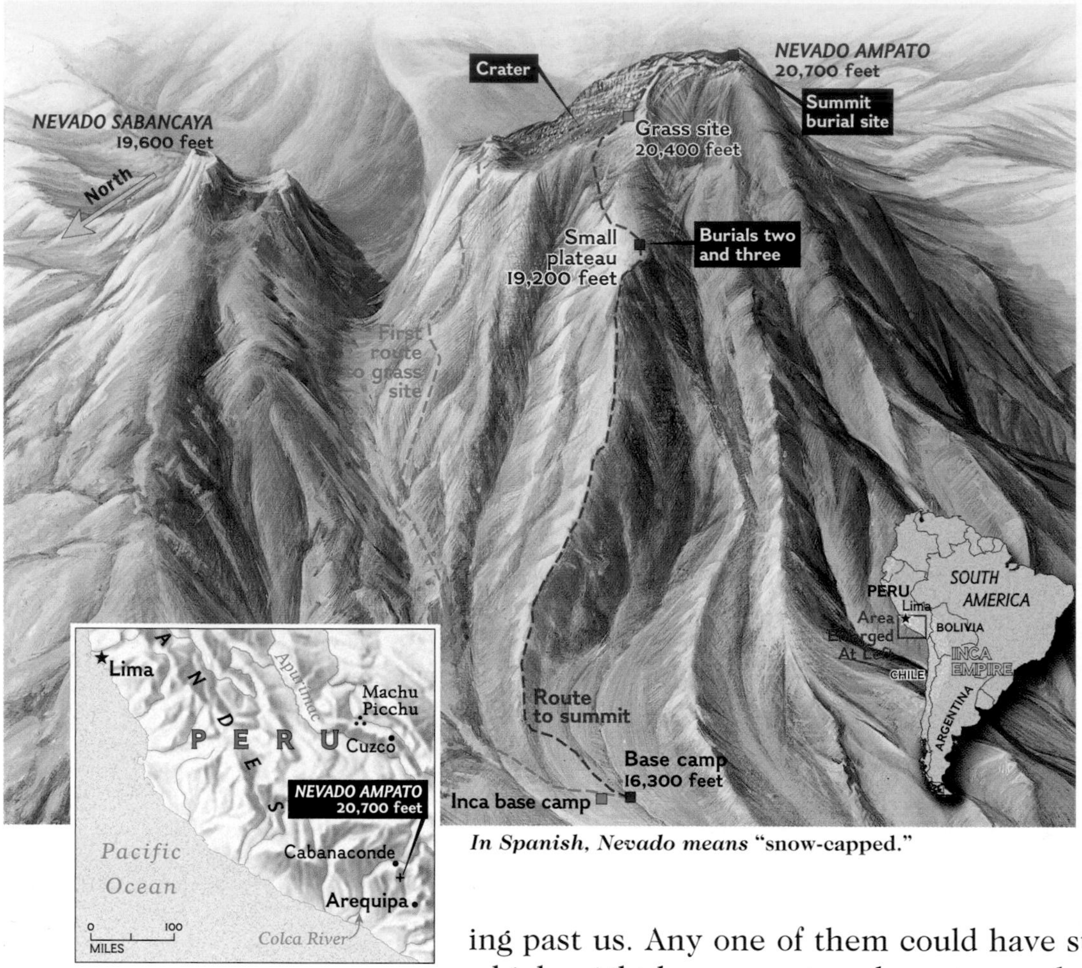

NEVADO AMPATO
20,700 feet
Crater
Summit
burial site
NEVADO SABANCAYA
19,600 feet
North
Grass site
20,400 feet
Small
plateau
19,200 feet
Burials two
and three
First
route
to grass
site
SOUTH
AMERICA
PERU
Lima
BOLIVIA
CHILE
INCA
EMPIRE
ARGENTINA
Route
to summit
Base camp
16,300 feet
Inca base camp
Lima
A N D E S
Apurímac
Machu
Picchu
P E R U
Cuzco
NEVADO AMPATO
20,700 feet
Pacific
Ocean
Cabanaconde
Arequipa
0
100
MILES
Colca River

In Spanish, Nevado means "snow-capped."

The highest point (20,700 feet) on the huge summit rim of Ampato had steep gullies leading down from it (right). The ice maiden was swept down one of the gullies when a part of the summit ridge collapsed.

It was too late in the day to reach Ampato's highest summit, which was about a mile away and 300 feet higher. But we were surprised to see that even it was not covered in snow.

Our problem now was getting back down to our camp and the safety of our tent. We decided to take a different way back. It would be quicker, but steeper and icier. As we descended, ice pinnacles blocked our path. While we walked, small rock slides went crashing past us. Any one of them could have started an avalanche, which might have swept us down to our deaths.

Nerves jangling, we finally crossed the lower part of that slope and two hours later reached our tent in the dark.

SEPTEMBER 7

The next day, using a different route along a ridge, we moved our tent up to a small plateau at 19,200 feet. There we found the remains of several Inca ruins, including wooden poles that could have been used to make large tents. After setting up our own tent, we searched for the route the Incas had used to the top. We found grass and pieces of wood that had been placed onto the steeper sections of the slope to help make a trail to the summit.

SEPTEMBER 8

The next morning we crossed over the "grass site" at 20,400 feet and made our way through and around ice pinnacles inside Ampato's crater until we were about 200 feet below the summit.

Miguel points to feathers sticking out of the steep slope on the summit of Ampato (left). The ice pinnacle-filled crater of Ampato is visible below (center). This is the first of the rare Inca statues found on the summit (right).

The frozen rock was steep and slippery, and we couldn't get up the summit's western side. We struggled on the eastern side. Finally I was just able to get over the worst part by pulling myself up with my ice ax.

I pulled Miguel up, too, and the rest of the way was a simple scramble up over ice and rock to the top.

Miguel's brother had climbed to the summit two years before. He told us the ridge was like he'd always seen it, over 30 feet wide and covered with ice. Now the ridge was only 3 feet wide. There was no layer of ice, just frozen ground covered by volcanic ash from Sabancaya.

I stopped to take notes while Miguel continued along the ridge. He whistled, and I looked up to see him with his ice ax raised.

When I reached him, he pointed without saying a word: Even from 40 feet away, it was possible to see reddish feathers sticking out near the top of the ridge. We had both seen feathers like this on Inca statues at other sites, and so we knew instantly they

would most likely be from a feathered headdress.

Although the feathers were only about 10 feet down from the top, the slope was steep and slippery—a mix of gravel and sand over ice. A slip would have meant certain death. Miguel weighed far less than I did, so I tied a long sling onto him and held him as he climbed down to uncover a statue made of a rare seashell, with a reddish feathered headdress. Nearby, also covered with gravel, were two more statues, one gold and one silver.

Their textiles were so well preserved, they looked new.

The feathers that had been exposed were still in good condition. This meant that the gravel in which the statues had been buried had fallen away only days before. Indeed, the statues could have fallen farther down the slope at any moment.

Back on the summit ridge, we saw stones that had formed a corner of a building. Most of the structure had fallen down one of two naturally formed gullies that dropped 200 feet to the inside of the crater. From the ridge we could not see where these led.

15

So I wrapped two stones in yellow plastic that I had carried in case we needed to mark our way. I threw a stone down each of the gullies, thinking "It'll be a miracle if we ever see them again."

We then climbed down off the ridge and scrambled our way around beneath it. We soon spotted yellow plastic below us where the rocky slope met the ice pinnacles where we had been climbing to the summit only a few hours before.

A little farther we saw what looked to us like a mummy bundle lying on the ice.

It seemed so unlikely to find a mummy out in the open, we literally couldn't believe our eyes. Miguel said, "Maybe it's a climber's backpack."

Only half joking, I replied, "Maybe it's a climber."

As we drew closer, I knew from the stripes on the cloth that it was probably a mummy bundle. This would mean only one thing: The Incas had performed a human sacrifice on the ridge top. The bundle containing the victim had been buried in the structure that had collapsed when part of the summit ridge crashed into the crater.

I knew that even a partially frozen body would be invaluable for science. A frozen body is like a time capsule, which allows scientists to look back into the past and find out things difficult to know otherwise—such as what foods were eaten, what diseases and bacteria existed, who was related to the mummy, where it came from, and much more.

I grew more excited as I remembered that only three frozen mummies had been recovered in all of South America.

Descending toward it, we found fragments of a torn textile. A seashell, two cloth bags containing food offerings (maize kernels and a maize cob), llama bones, and pieces of Inca pottery were strewn about on the slope above the bundle.

After I photographed these items, Miguel used his ice ax to cut loose the bundle from the ice.

He turned it on its side for a better grip. Both of us were momentarily stunned as the body turned.

Miguel descends. Items were strewn about the slope (left). The mummy bundle was lying in the open amidst ice pinnacles, where it had come to rest after falling down from the summit (right).

Once the bundle was freed from the ice, we saw the ice maiden's face for the first time.

We looked straight into the face of a young girl.

She was the first *frozen* female mummy found in South America!

Her dried-out features made me fear that we had arrived too late. However, the bundle weighed about 90 pounds, which meant the body was still frozen. A dried-out mummy would have weighed much less.

I wondered what to do next. If we left the mummy behind in the open, the sun and volcanic ash would cause further damage. Climbers might find her and take her and the other artifacts as souvenirs or to sell. The ground was frozen rock hard, and it was impossible to bury the mummy. A heavy snowfall could cover the summit and make recovery impossible....

Thoughts rushed through my mind. It could take weeks, if not months, to get a government permit that would allow me to return and recover the mummy. Obtaining the funding to organize a scientific expedition could take even longer.

I decided that we should try to carry the mummy and the statues down the mountain. This would be difficult under the best of circumstances. Unfortunately, we were both feeling weak, and I had an upset stomach.

Just as I thought things couldn't be worse, it began to snow! Then, in the darkening light, Sabancaya erupted. We'd seen the volcano erupt before, but now it looked threatening.

Brushing aside a feeling of dread, we wrapped the bundle in plastic and attached it to my backpack. We had to scramble for a mile around the ice pinnacles inside the crater to link up with the route back to camp.

This was one of the hardest things I've ever done. My backpack was so heavy that any slip meant a hard fall, and I crashed to the ground a dozen times. I could only get back on my feet by propping myself against the ground with my ice ax and lunging upward. Every fall meant precious minutes lost.

Instead of its getting easier once we were out of the crater, the way became more dangerous. Cutting footholds immediately below me, Miguel feared that I would fall on him with the heavy load and that we would both be swept off the mountain.

Our headlamps barely lit the steep slope of mixed ice and gravel. Finally I realized it was foolish to continue. We left the mummy amidst some ice pinnacles at 19,900 feet.

It took us two hours to descend to our tent 700 feet below and crawl exhausted into our sleeping bags.

The next morning was clear and sunny. I returned alone to get the mummy, while Miguel took the equipment to our base camp. He and our burro driver met me at high camp and we descended to the base of the mountain. All along the way, I kept thinking about a problem.

How could we keep the mummy frozen?

It would take us a full day to reach the village of Cabanaconde, and from there we had to get to the city of Arequipa. Only in the city would we be able to keep the mummy permanently frozen by placing her in a freezer. The thought struck me that we had something that would work in the meantime: our sleeping pads. They would provide insulation from the heat of the sun just as they had from the cold ground.

We wrapped the mummy bundle in the pads before loading it on a burro. "Why are you covering the burro's eyes?" I asked the burro driver. "Because he will run off if he senses that he is being loaded with a dead body," the driver explained.

The thought of the burro's running off across the countryside with the mummy kept us alert as we continued our way down to spend the night near a stream at 15,300 feet.

Wrapped in insulated pads to protect her from the sun, the mummy is taken to safety.

The central plaza of Arequipa is one of the most beautiful in Peru. The city has about a million inhabitants and is the current home of the ice maiden.

SEPTEMBER 10

The next morning we began a 13-hour, non-stop trek—except for ten minutes to share a single tin of sardines—to Cabanaconde.

Fortunately we hiked mostly above 14,000 feet. By the time we started the descent to the village it was nighttime and cool. When our headlamp batteries wore out, we stumbled on in the dark. We knew that a bus would be leaving the village that night and that it would reach Arequipa before sunup.

We could keep the mummy frozen if we hurried.

At last, we placed the bundle in the undercarriage of the bus, where it was cooler.

When the mummy reached Arequipa the next morning with

ice still attached to it, we had a tremendous feeling of satisfaction. Our efforts of the previous few days had been successful.

The mummy and other artifacts were taken to Catholic University. I had worked before with Professor José Antonio Chávez, dean of the Archaeology Department, and he became co-director of the project.

Thanks to the tireless efforts of Professor Chávez and archaeologist Ruth Salas, a laboratory was quickly established so that work could begin.

Mummy specialists from several countries were consulted. Some of them came to Arequipa to help answer such questions as: What is the best way to conserve the frozen body? How should we proceed with work on it?

23

The textiles would have to be treated differently from the body. They were extremely rare and important in their own right. Some specialists recommended removing them immediately. Although it would be difficult, we would have to take them off without damaging the skin tissue.

Meanwhile, Professor Chávez and I knew we had to return to the mountain as quickly as possible. The discovery could break into the news at any moment, leading treasure hunters to the sites. Or the weather could change, making a scientific investigation of the archaeological remains on the mountain difficult, if not impossible. The National Institute of Culture assisted us by allowing a permit to be issued faster than normal, and the National Geographic Society provided the necessary funding. Within a month we were headed back to the mountain.

As we left, one scientist, caught up with problems posed by the first frozen body, only half-jokingly said, "Please don't bring back any more mummies."

This possibility seemed so remote that we laughed.

Little did we know.

The silver female Inca statue (upper left) and rare gold female statue (right) were found at the ice maiden's burial place. The colorful feathers of the female Inca shell figurine (lower left) first drew our attention on the summit of Ampato.

24

I hiked out of Cabanaconde on October 7 with a team now numbering over 20 people, including archaeologists from Catholic University and a National Geographic film crew. To carry all the food and equipment, we needed a total of 30 burros and horses.

By October 11 we had 18 people living near the Inca ruins at 19,200 feet. More importantly, our team had already located two more human sacrificial burials! One of these was especially significant. Shawl pins indicated that the body was that of a female, while her small size suggested that she was young. She was wearing a feather headdress and was surrounded by nearly 40 beautifully preserved ceramics of purely Inca origin.

We chose to work in the burial site without gloves so that we had a greater sensitivity and could avoid damaging any exposed textiles. As we dug around the mummy, our fingertips became cracked and sore.

A much larger expedition, barely visible in the photo, returned to Ampato (left). The team's base camp at 16,300 feet was built in a dry gully, to protect the tents from the high winds (above).

Excavating an Inca burial site at 19,200 feet, the team observes an eruption of Sabancaya (above).

Although the simplest task—even tying a shoelace—could cause grimaces of pain, the excitement of slowly uncovering rare artifacts kept us going. Weaving tools, wooden spoons, a wooden box, small wooden ceremonial drinking vessels, cloth bundles containing offerings, and other items emerged. Each added to our growing knowledge of the burial. A pair of tiny sandals made us stop to reflect on the fate of this young child.

After three days we were finally able to free the body and lift it out of its frozen tomb. The body had been there, sitting on a flat stone, for 500 years. It was a surprisingly emotional event.

In the past, some of us had been together on difficult expeditions that had not led to discoveries of special importance. Now

we had done a complete excavation at the site of one of the most important Inca ceremonies. We worked at over 19,000 feet, making this one of the world's highest archaeological excavations.

Arcadio Mamani, one of our climbing assistants, made ritual offerings to the mountain gods. As the only man from the Colca Valley to be with us at this high altitude, he felt a special responsibility to the deity many of his people believe lives in the mountain. "Nothing should be taken from the mountain without something being given in return," he said, and we all agreed.

We carved an ice cave to hold the mummy bundle, to preserve it in a frozen state until we left the mountain.

Meanwhile, new discoveries were being made.

The first burial we excavated at 19,200 feet provided the spectacular discovery of an Inca mummy with a headdress (one of only a few known) and one of the finest collections of Inca pottery ever found.

On the first trip Miguel and I found wooden poles at this site. Now remnants of a grass flooring were uncovered along with pieces of textiles and artifacts at two places that had been surrounded by the poles. Clearly the poles had supported tents. The Spaniards described the Incas as using tents, but to our knowledge these poles are the first tent remains ever discovered.

Orlando Jain, Ruddy Perea, and Walter Diaz, archaeology students at Catholic University, showed me a tomb they had worked on where skeletal remains had been charred. By amazing chance, lightning had struck the mummy after it had been buried at this high point of the small plateau.

The lack of shawl pins and the discovery of a male statue beneath the mummy's skeleton suggested that these were the remains of a male child.

Could it have been sacrificed as a companion to the girl nearby? Were both sacrificed to serve as companions to the first mummy?

Throughout the Andes, lightning represents the power of the mountain gods. Mountain gods are said to use it to kill those who offend them or to strike down their livestock. They also use lightning to empower people who will become priests.

I thought about this as I walked alone among the ruins. Never before have so many human sacrifices been found on a single mountain. Was Ampato especially significant to the Incas? I wondered what still lay waiting to be discovered and what the site would look like when we were next able to return to it. Visions of the scattered remains of looted sites I'd seen elsewhere filled my mind. I could only hope some better fate was in store for this important site.

This picture of me was taken as we got ready to take the mummy found in the first burial at 19,200 feet back to Arequipa.

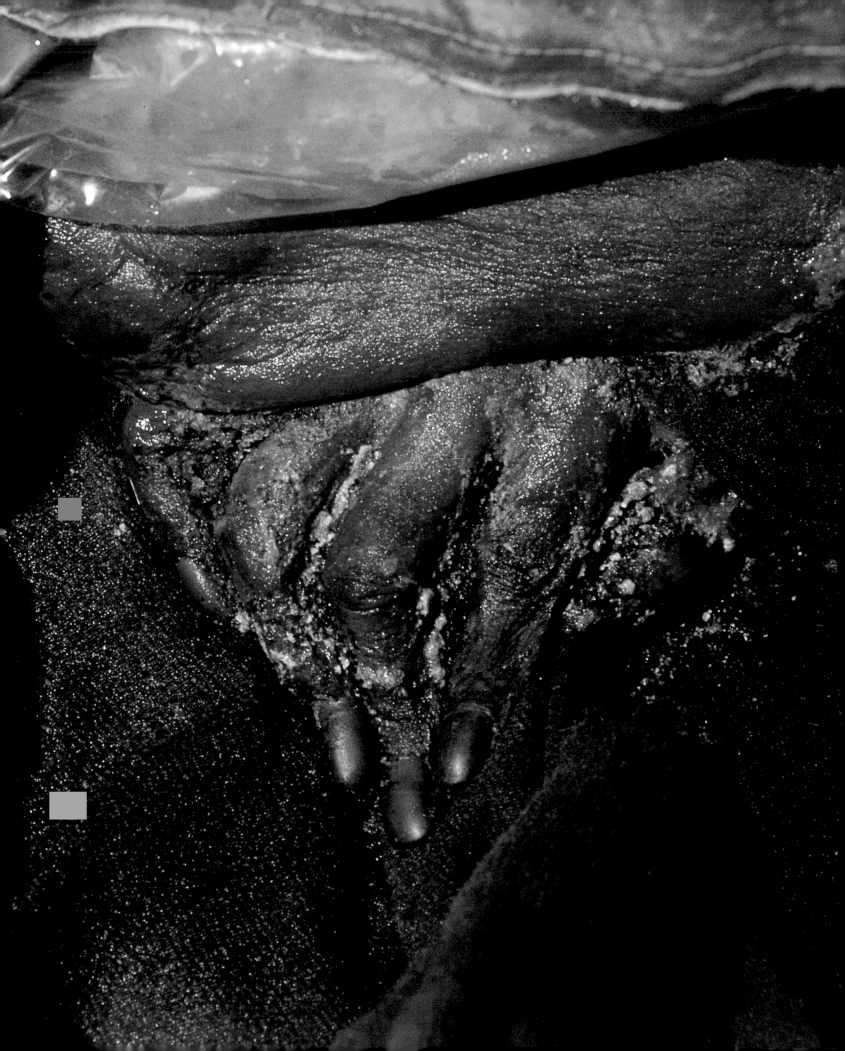

O nce back in Arequipa we were met by a team of specialists who had worked on the famous 5,000-year-old Tyrolean "Iceman" in Austria. The first mummy found on Ampato had come to be called the "ice maiden" and was also nicknamed "Juanita."

After examining her, Dr. Konrad Spindler of the University of Innsbruck said, "Your mummy is better preserved than the Iceman, and this makes it a discovery of worldwide importance." He was being modest: The Iceman is about 4,500 years older than the Inca ice maiden and is unique in the world. But his comments underscored the significance of the Ampato finds.

Our team began work on the ice maiden. We'd found the outer wrapping of the mummy bundle scattered in fragments above it during the first expedition. The second wrapping had also been damaged in the fall, but was nonetheless fairly complete. It may have been made locally. Repairs in the sewing made us think that perhaps the wrapping even belonged to the girl.

T he ice maiden's hand is tightly clutching her dress against her side (left). Ice was still attached to her when she first reached the city of Arequipa, just before she was placed in a freezer (above).

The X-ray of the ice maiden's skull also showed the presence of shawl pins, and this was our first proof that the mummy was a girl (upper). This gold pin was in the lap of the female mummy found in the first burial at 19,200 feet. The damage caused by a lightning strike can clearly be seen (lower).

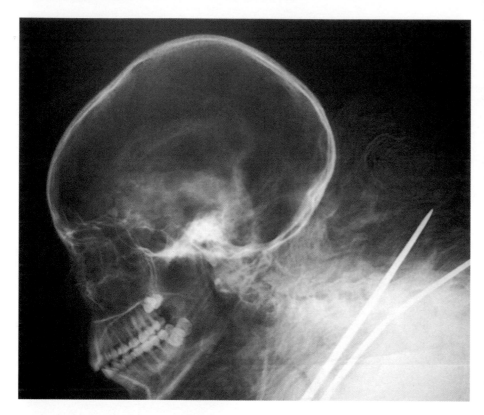

The tension that sometimes reigned in the laboratory could be high. There were times when the lab team would be in great spirits and full of jokes, but there were also periods when work was so intense that people would be startled by a cough.

Blankets of ice were placed around the areas of the mummy not being worked upon. The surface temperatures of exposed parts of the body were constantly monitored to ensure that the ice maiden never came close to thawing.

When a small cloth bundle that had been placed along Juanita's side was opened, we saw clumps of hair. They looked like clippings from a child's first haircut. Keeping such hair was a widespread Andean custom. We also found a carved piece of seashell on a cord, a belt, and a small cloth bag. All of these were most likely personal items belonging to the girl. Another feather-covered bag found with Juanita contained coca leaves. They were, and still are, sacred offerings.

One vivid red and yellow piece of Juanita's clothing caused

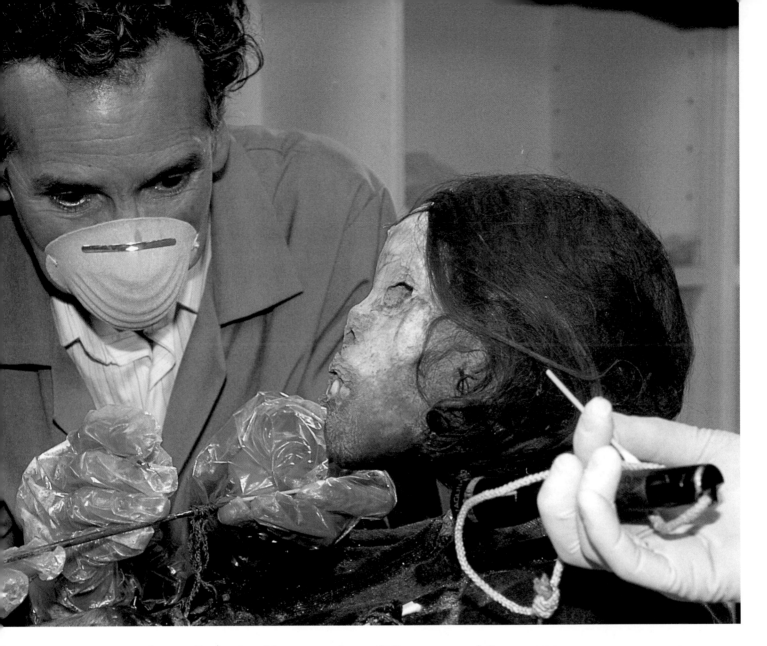

Work begins on the ice maiden to remove her outer clothing.

textile specialist William Conklin to exclaim, "This is one of the finest Inca women's textiles in the world." It had been beautifully made of alpaca wool.

As work proceeded, the girl's pigtail appeared, tied by a thread to her waistband. Obviously she had been clothed, at least in part, by others, just before, or very soon after, she died. Gold and silver shawl pins were connected to woven cords, with miniature wood carvings attached to them: A box, two vessels, and what looked like a dog or fox were amidst these precious carvings.

Although many shawl pins have been found with female burials in the past, none had such items attached to them.

Once the clothing was removed from around the girl's shoulders and from above her folded arms, she became much more a distinct human being to us all.

For some team members, she even had her own personality. One person said, "When I've had problems, she has come to me in my dreams and advised me on what to do."

Her humanity especially hit home when we uncovered her right hand and found it holding the cloth in a firm grip. By grasping the textile so tightly, she had made it a seemingly impossible task to remove the cloth without damaging her skin.

This meant the temporary termination of our work, but thanks to Mr. Conklin we had accomplished one of our principal goals. By making calculations and laboriously piecing together the data, he was able to reconstruct exactly how the girl had been clothed. She had been dressed very much like the female statues that accompanied her.

We had found four of the female statues with their clothing perfectly intact. The meticulously woven miniature textiles amazed us. One was made of top-quality wool from a vicuna, a wild camel-like animal. "Its weave count is as high as the finest machine-made clothing," said Professor Chávez.

We knew that the third mummy had been struck by lightning, but we had high hopes that the second mummy, which wore the feathered headdress, would be better preserved than Juanita; perhaps it would even be completely frozen.

Given the lavish amount of fine Inca pottery found near her, we were surprised that the girl's textiles were so common.

The ice maiden's shawl is one of the best-preserved Inca female textiles ever recovered. The brilliant colors are still visible (below). In the artist's rendering of the ice maiden, the headdress found with the mummy at 19,200 feet and the dress without the shawl have been pictured (right).

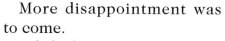

More disappointment was to come.

While loosening the head cloth, I shined my flashlight between one of the folds—and saw only the charred bones of a skeleton. This mummy, like the third one, must have been hit by lightning.

Somehow the lightning had burned the flesh of the child, but only scorched the textiles where they came in contact with metal objects, such as the shawl pins.

Thanks to the finds made at Ampato and our knowledge of Inca ceremonies in general, we have a reasonable idea of how the Incas conducted human sacrificial rituals on the volcano.

A procession must have started out from the valley below, stopping at way stations. Priests and their assistants would have led the pilgrimage with llamas carrying supplies of wood, grass, blankets, pottery, food, and ritual offerings, including the human victim, usually a child.

The people probably danced and sang as they walked to the foot of Ampato. They most likely would have waited here while the priests and their helpers began their ascent to the site at 19,200 feet.

Juanita would probably have spent the night in one of the tents there, while the priests made offerings of beverages and food-stuffs. The procession would then have climbed to the "grass summit," where another rest was taken and further offerings made. The climb is so high and steep that Juanita may have had to be carried to this point.

Rather than thinking that they were simply killing someone, the Incas believed that the child would enter a glorious afterlife with the gods. Later, offerings would have been made to the child, asking for help in dealing with the gods. And so it was considered a great honor to be sacrificed.

However, during the ascent Juanita must have felt some fear of her approaching death. The altitude would have helped dull her mind. Perhaps she was given a ritual alcoholic drink of maize beer just prior to her sacrifice.

Certainly she died while on the summit itself, either as she was being wrapped in her bundle of textiles or soon after, when she was buried inside the stone structure. The offerings of items such as the statues would have been placed carefully under, around, and even above her while prayers were offered to the gods of the land, the sky, and the underworld. With the completion of this ceremony, the people would have felt that they had fulfilled their obligation to the gods and would in return receive favors from them.

Some historical accounts stress that human sacrifices were rare and took place only during major state events, such as the death of an emperor. But it seems logical to me that very practical local concerns led to sacrifices.

A lengthy period of extreme drought and/or volcanic eruptions similar to those Sabancaya is making today would have caused great hardship. Droughts and volcanic ash kill plants being grown for food. They also pollute or deplete the water sources needed for life.

The Incas believed that those they sacrificed would appeal directly to the gods to stop the volcano's fire or bring the rain.

Villagers reenact the procession to Ampato. A traditional curer leads the group and is wearing clothes like that of an Inca priest (above). A young girl reenacts the ice maiden offering maize beer to the gods, a ritual that still takes place in the Andes today (right).

In May 1996, a police motorcade accompanied the ice maiden to the Arequipa airport. It was a procession worthy of a princess—and this seemed only appropriate. Packed in a special container inside a larger case containing dry ice, she was being transported to Washington, D.C.

On May 13, 1996, she was taken in a van to the Department of Radiology at Johns Hopkins University Hospital. There some of the world's most advanced technology awaited her.

I felt a strange mixture of anticipation, a sense of accomplishment, and a feeling of wonder. Images of finding her lying on the top of a field of ice were fused with what was happening before my eyes: The ice maiden was in a white operating room, surrounded by robed and masked doctors who were working in front of a bank of instruments and computer screens.

It was after 2 a.m., but Dr. Elliot Fishman of the Department of Radiology was still receiving data from one of the latest model CAT scan units. These units allow three-dimensional images to show the internal soft tissue and bones without touching them. They could even be moved and turned around and sliced in pieces, all on the computer.

The computer program Dr. Fishman was working with was the kind used for making Jurassic Park.

An Inca jug for holding ceremonial beer shows the result of a lightning strike—pumice fused to its handle (left). A silver figurine of a llama was found at 19,200 feet. Llamas carried supplies up to the site and would also sometimes be sacrificed to the gods (above).

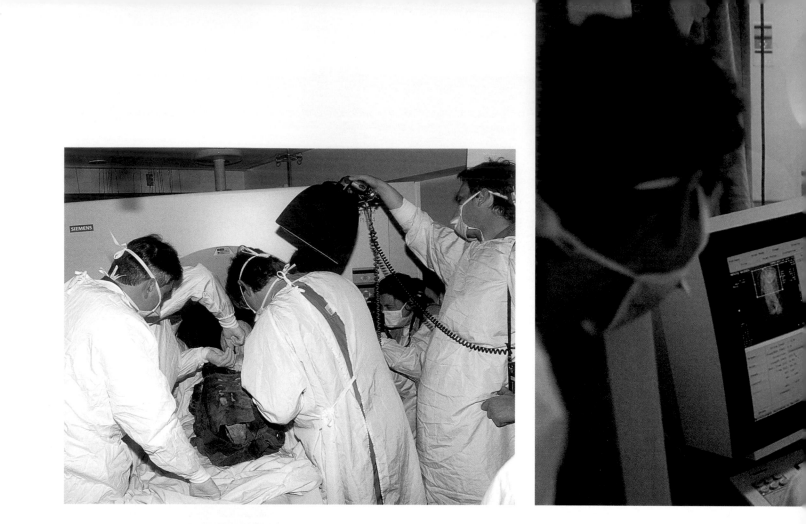

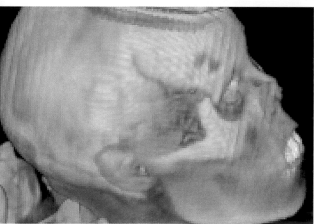

Scientists at Johns Hopkins Hospital in Baltimore take a sample of tissue from the ice maiden by using a special needle (upper left). The fracture that caused the ice maiden's death can be seen leading from her right eye in this CAT scan taken at Johns Hopkins Hospital (lower left).

For more than an hour we could not take our eyes from the computer screen.

Wearing glasses adapted for 3-D viewing, we could see the ice maiden's textiles being removed by computer and could examine the condition of her internal organs. In 3-D the images seemed to leap from the screen, and in one of them we were even able to enter the inside of the skull and look out!

Then Dr. Fishman pointed to a new discovery. "Look at the fracture by the right eye," he said, enlarging it on the screen. "Clearly she had been hit with a sharp blow to the head." The evidence of internal bleeding and the lack of any healing indicated that this was most likely the cause of her death.

Everyone present grew silent as the stark reality sank in. The girl would have been dazed due to exhaustion and the altitude, and a blow to the head would have meant a quick death.

A tiny piece of tissue taken by a special needle from the girl's stomach yielded more information. "She must have eaten a meal of vegetables within six to eight hours before dying," said Dr. Edward McCarthy, a renowned pathologist at Johns Hopkins.

The girl showed no signs of malnutrition, no bone diseases were found, and she had normal skeletal growth.

To preserve the body, conservation specialists agreed that the humidity should be as close to 100 percent as possible and the

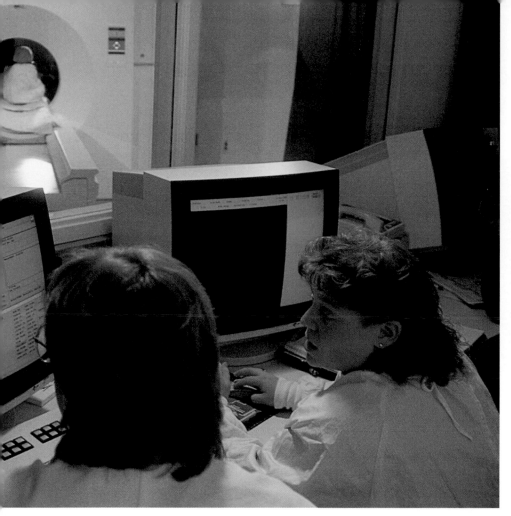

temperature should be at least as low as 0°F. Even at temperatures well below freezing, chemical processes continue in organic matter. These processes need to be slowed down as much as possible so the body can remain well preserved throughout the centuries.

Before the ice maiden had reached the United States, a custom-made unit—and a spare—had been built by the Carrier Corporation, experts in air-conditioning technology. The case allows the temperature and humidity to be controlled and constantly monitored by computer. If the temperature rises too high, both sound and light alarms go off. An electrical shortage also sets off alarms, and a back-up generator is ready to provide the necessary current. At the same time, the unit is movable and allows a full view of the mummy.

Once the mummy was in the case, technical and conservation specialists needed to observe both for a few weeks.

Realizing this, Peruvian scientists and government officials, together with the National Geographic Society, agreed to exhibit the ice maiden in Washington, D.C., before returning her to Peru.

More than 80,000 people of all ages saw her in less than a month at Explorers Hall in the National Geographic Society.

When she returned to Arequipa she had a royal welcome, and both military and local bands played. Nearly 100,000 people

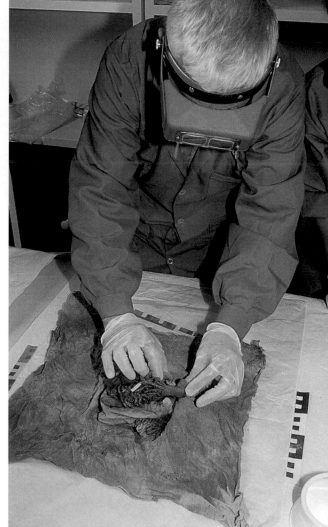

Doctors at Johns Hopkins Hospital examine computerized images of the CAT scan being taken of the ice maiden (center). A bundle containing personal items of the ice maiden is carefully opened. The outer cloth was later found to contain the pollen of 17 plants (above).

lined up to see her during the following months.

Results of studies undertaken by scientists in several countries are gradually being received and analyzed.

Dr. Alex Chepstow-Lusty of the Department of Plant Scientists at Cambridge University in England, has identified the pollen of 17 plants found in the cloth used to carry Juanita's personal items.

The Institute for Genomic Research in Rockville, Maryland performed the delicate process of extracting the ice maiden's DNA. Dr. Keith McKenney told me, "We were able to obtain the best DNA profile known from ancient times." The ice maiden was unique in having as much DNA in the tested areas as a living person! Not only that, but she had a variant in her DNA that has never been reported before. This means that we can better compare her DNA with that of other individuals, both past and present.

We can even find her relatives who are living today. Somewhere in Peru there are girls Juanita's age who are related to her!

Dr. Irv Taylor of the Radiocarbon Laboratory of the University of California, Riverside, estimated her lifetime by examining the carbon 14 in her hair. His research showed that the ice maiden lived 530 years ago (plus or minus 50 years). This means that she lived around A.D. 1470—just before the time that Columbus landed in America.

Based on a study of her dental growth by Dr. John Verano of Tulane University, we know that Juanita was about 14 years old when she died.

If she had lived in recent times, she would have been in high school. But 500 years ago she was already a young woman whose destiny was to be sacrificed to the gods.

For centuries she lay forgotten. Then in 1995 she was found, and once again she has been honored. Young people from around the world write to me about the ice maiden. They are fascinated by her.

Because she was so young herself, and is so lifelike, she has become for many a personal link to the Inca culture.

A tiny sandal (upper), an Inca pot (middle), and a spiny oyster shell were found with the female buried at 19,200 feet. The ice maiden was about 14 when she died (right).

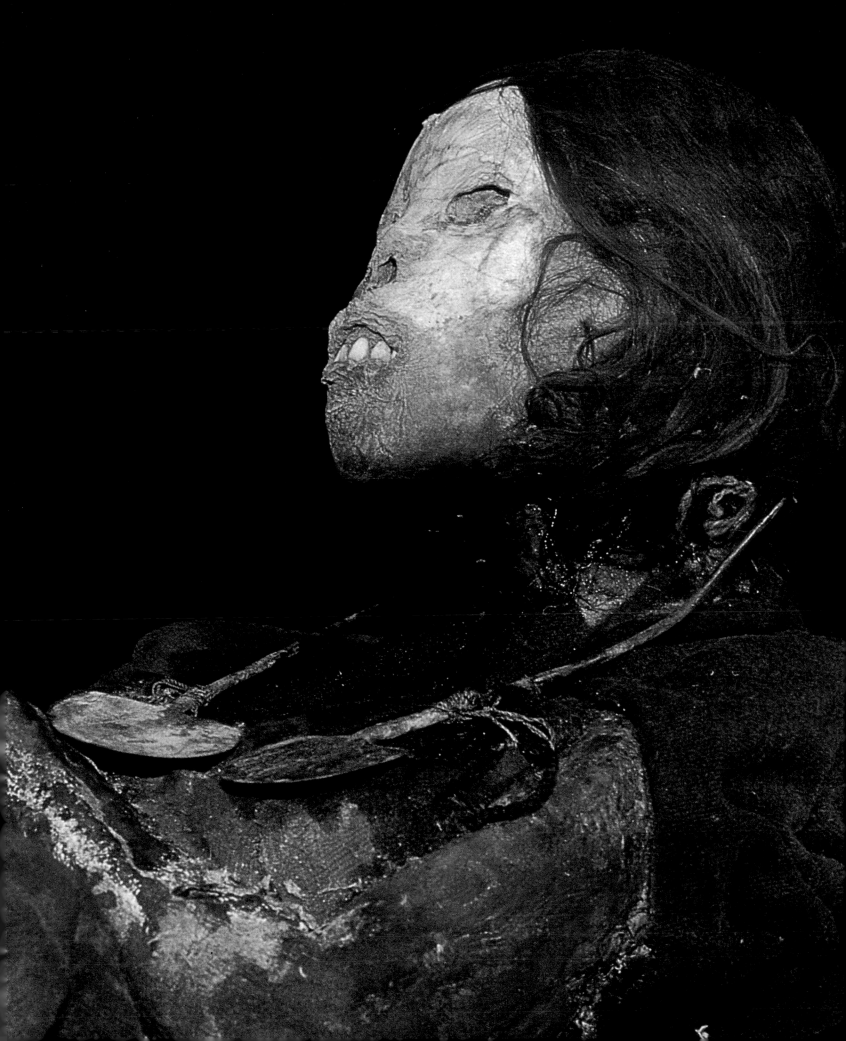

ca. A.D. 1200–1438	Beginning of Inca Civilization in what is now Peru, and reign of the "legendary Incas."
ca. 1200	Genghis Khan and Mongols begin conquering Asia.
1215	Magna Carta is signed in England.
1325	The Aztec founded their capital in Mexico.
1431	Joan of Arc burned at the stake in France.
ca. 1438-1471	Reign of Inca emperor Pachacuti.
ca. 1470	Inca ice maiden described in this book was sacrificed.
1492	Columbus discovers the "New World," America.
1471–1493	Reign of Tupa Inca Yupanqui.
1498	Vasco da Gama makes the first European voyage to India.
ca. 1500	Italian Renaissance begins (Leonardo da Vinci, Michelangelo).
ca. 1510	First Africans brought to America as slaves.
1513	Balboa discovers the Pacific Ocean.
1519	Cortés begins conquest of the Aztec Empire. Magellan sets sail for the Pacific (1519-1521).
1521	Beginning of Protestant Reformation in Europe (Martin Luther).
1493–1527	Reign of Inca emperor Huayna Capac.
ca. 1527	The Spanish explorer Francisco Pizarro discovers the Inca Empire.
1532	November 16, 1532, Pizarro captures Atahuallpa, last Inca King of Peru, and slaughters his army. Signals the coming end of the Inca Empire.
1620	The Pilgrims land in America.

Altitude • a high level or elevation above a surface; a position at a height.

Anthropology • the study of humans; at the university level generally divided into linguistics, archaeology, and cultural and physical anthropology.

Archaeology • the study of the material remains of peoples and cultures of the past; a subdivision of anthropology.

Artifact • an object remaining from a particular period, something created by humans, usually for a practical purpose.

Carbon-14 dating • dating done by finding out how much decay has taken place in carbon 14, which decays at a precise rate once a living being dies.

CAT scan • an image made by an instrument that combines X-ray and computer technology.

Conquistador • a leader in the Spanish conquest of America, especially of Mexico and Peru, in the 16th century.

Crater • a bowl-shaped or hollowed-out area produced by a volcanic eruption (or by the impact of a meteorite).

Culture • the entire way of life shared by a group of people.

DNA • (short for deoxyribonucleic acid), a substance found in every cell in a person's body, which defines unique characteristics, such as what a person looks like. Most of the DNA is found in the cell's nucleus, but some is found outside the nucleus in structures within the cell called mitochondria. Mitochondrial DNA is easier to find in the cells of mummies and is passed on only by the mother's side of the family.

Genomic • referring to the genetic material of an organism.

Ice pinnacles • formations of ice, shaped into a vertical, tapering form by erosion.

Mountain • usually defined as a landform rising at least 1,000 feet above the surrounding area.

Mummy • a body that is either treated for burial with preservatives in the manner of the ancient Egyptians or that is unusually well-preserved.

Pathologist • a scientist who interprets changes caused by diseases in tissues and body fluids.

Summit • the highest point attainable on a mountain; may also be used to refer to other prominent points on a mountain.

Volcano • a vent in the crust of the earth, usually shaped like a mountain, that can produce heat, molten rock, or steam.

X-ray • a type of radiation that can penetrate a solid substance and produce photographs from under the substance's surface.

Illustrations are indicated in **boldface**. If illustrations are included within a page span, the entire span is **boldface**.

The world's largest nonprofit scientific and educational organization, the National Geographic Society was founded in 1888 "for the increase and diffusion of geographic knowledge." Fulfilling this mission, the Society educates and inspires millions every day through magazines, books, television programs, videos, maps and atlases, research grants, the National Geography Bee, teacher workshops, and innovative classroom materials.

Visit our website at www.nationalgeographic.com.

The Society is supported through membership dues and income from the sale of its educational products. Call 1-800-NGS-LINE for more information.